Welcome to the Castle!

This is a brave knight called Henry.

And this is Willow, his horse.

Solve the puzzles in this book and help Henry find the king's golden shield.

Look out for Finley the falcon too. You'll find him in every picture!

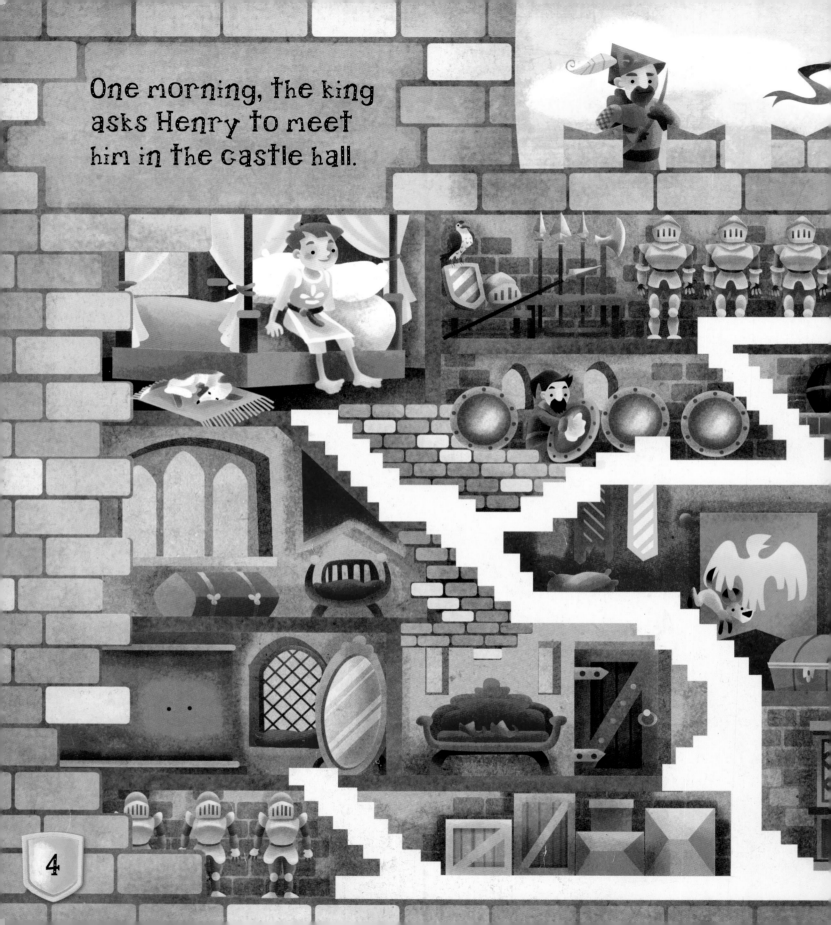

One morning, the king asks Henry to meet him in the castle hall.

4

Can you help Henry get to the hall?

Can you spot these things?

three dogs

a pair of slippers

two boys

5

"I want you to find the golden shield," says the king. "I lost it in the Great Cave long ago."

Can you spot these things?

two fried eggs

a cat

the king's cup

6

Can you match the other shields to their swords?

7

Henry and Willow set off on their quest.

Can you find four differences between the two castle guards?

Can you spot these things?
a family of ducks

a peacock

hobby horse

9

Henry meets a group of knights.

"Don't go to the Great Cave!" one says.
"A scary dragon lives there now."

Which knight looks different from his friends?

Can you spot these things?

a cottage

a goat

three sheep

11

But Henry likes all animals —
even dragons — so he carries on.

Which path should he take to the cave?

Can you spot these things?

two fish

three pine trees

a woodcutter

13

When he gets to the Great Cave, Henry throws his sword and shield into the bushes.

He doesn't want to scare the dragon.

Can you spot these things?

a fox

two butterflies

three blue flowers

14

Can you see where the sword and shield are?

The dragon sees Henry and roars a terrible, fiery roar. All the animals run away.

But Henry isn't scared. "I don't want to fight," he says. "Look, I haven't even got a sword."

Can you spot these things?

a bird

two white flowers

two toadstools

18

Two deer are watching from the trees. Can you spot four differences between them?

The dragon is amazed.

"Knights always want to fight me!" he says. "Until I scare them away!"

Some of the knights ran away so fast they left their flags behind.

Which two flags are the same?

Can you spot these things?

a spider's web

a knight's glove

two owls

21

Henry explains about the king's lost shield.

"Come with me," says the dragon, and takes Henry into the cave.

Can you spot these things?

two bats

two rings

three candles

22

Can you help Henry and the dragon find the shield?

23

"Let's take the shield back together!" says the dragon. "You ride and I'll fly!"

24

Can you see four other things flying in the sky?

Can you spot these things?

three cows

a windmill

a swan

25

The king is very pleased to have his shield back. That night, he holds a banquet for two very special guests.

One of them is Henry.

Can you spot these things?

three juggling balls

two jugs

a recorder

26

Who is the other special guest?
And what do you think is his
favourite food?

Answers

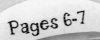

Pages 4-5

Follow the red line to the castle hall.

Pages 6-7

The matching swords and shields are connected with lines.

Pages 8-9

The four differences are circled in red.

Pages 10-11

The circled knight is wearing a red sword and trousers, and his visor is down.

Pages 12-13

The red line leads to the Great Cave.

Pages 14-15

Henry's sword and shield are circled in red.

Pages 16-17

The matching rabbits are connected with red lines.

Pages 18-19

The four differences are circled in red.

Answers

Pages 20-21

The matching flags are circled in red.

Pages 22-23

Finley

Follow the red line to the golden shield.

Finley

30

Pages 24-25

Pages 26-27

Finley

Finley

The four flying objects are a kite, a duck, a white bird and a hot air balloon. They are circled in red.

The special guest is the dragon, and his favourite food is strawberries!

More knightly fun

Knight day!
Dress up as a knight for the day! Make a knight's tunic out of an old pillow case. After you've asked permission, cut semi-circles in the folds for your head and arms. Wear it over trousers and a long-sleeved top with a belt around your waist. Maybe you could even have a knight-themed party!

Make a castle
Use a big cardboard box for the castle and tape cardboard tubes to the corners for towers. Ask an adult to cut around the top of the box to make battlements and to cut out a door and some slit windows, too. If you have any toy knights or horses, you could play with them in your castle.

Design your own shield
Draw the outline of a big shield on some paper and use pens, paints or crayons to add your own design. A knight's shield often showed something about who he was or where he lived, so try to make your design say something about you. You could make a pattern out of your initials, or draw something that's near your home, like a tree or a bridge.

Make a dragon puppet
Draw the side of a dragon's head and the end of its tail on some thin card. Cut them out and tape a pencil to the back of each. Cut a long strip of paper for the dragon's body. Fold it backwards and forwards like a concertina, then tape one end to the head and the other to the tail. Move the pencils to make your dragon move.